The Pacific Typographical Society and the California Gold Rush of 1849

Also from Westphalia Press
westphaliapress.org

The Idea of the Digital University

Dialogue in the Roman-Greco World

The History of Photography

International or Local Ownership?: Security Sector Development in Post-Independent Kosovo

Lankes, His Woodcut Bookplates

Opportunity and Horatio Alger

The Role of Theory in Policy Analysis

Natural Gas as an Instrument of Russian State Power

Non Profit Organizations and Disaster

The Idea of Neoliberalism: The Emperor Has Threadbare Contemporary Clothes

Social Satire and the Modern Novel

Ukraine vs. Russia: Revolution, Democracy and War: Selected Articles and Blogs, 2010-2016

James Martineau and Rebuilding Theology

A Strategy for Implementing the Reconciliation Process

Issues in Maritime Cyber Security

Growing Inequality: Bridging Complex Systems, Population Health and Health Disparities

Designing, Adapting, Strategizing in Online Education

Gunboat and Gun-runner

Pacific Hurtgen: The American Army in Northern Luzon, 1945

New Frontiers in Criminology

Understanding Art

Homeopathy

Fishing the Florida Keys

Iran: Who Is Really In Charge?

Contracting, Logistics, Reverse Logistics: The Project, Program and Portfolio Approach

The Thomas Starr King Dispute

Springfield: The Novel

Alchemy: Ancient and Modern

Lariats and Lassos

Mr. Garfield of Ohio

The French Foreign Legion

War in Syria

Naturism Comes to the United States

Feeding the Global South

The History of Men's Raiment

The Pacific Typographical Society and the California Gold Rush of 1849

A Forgotten Chapter in the History of Typographical Unionism in America

by Douglas C. McMurtrie

WESTPHALIA PRESS
An imprint of Policy Studies Organization

The Pacific Typographical Society and the California Gold Rush of 1849:
A Forgotten Chapter in the History of Typographical Unionism in America
All Rights Reserved © 2017 by Policy Studies Organization

Westphalia Press
An imprint of Policy Studies Organization
1527 New Hampshire Ave., NW
Washington, D.C. 20036
info@ipsonet.org

ISBN-13: 978-1-63391-614-2
ISBN-10: 1-63391-614-6

Cover design by Jeffrey Barnes:
jbarnesbook.design

Daniel Gutierrez-Sandoval, Executive Director
PSO and Westphalia Press

Updated material and comments on this edition
can be found at the Westphalia Press website:
www.westphaliapress.org

THE PACIFIC TYPOGRAPHICAL SOCIETY AND THE CALIFORNIA GOLD RUSH OF 1849

THE PACIFIC TYPOGRAPHICAL SOCIETY AND THE CALIFORNIA GOLD RUSH OF 1849

A Forgotten Chapter in the History of Typographical Unionism in America

By

DOUGLAS C. McMURTRIE

CHICAGO, ILLINOIS
LUDLOW TYPOGRAPH COMPANY
MCMXXVIII

This booklet is Ludlow-set in Nicolas Jenson and printed direct from slugs. The cover design is made up of Ludlow ornament, and also printed from slugs.

THE PACIFIC TYPOGRAPHICAL SOCIETY AND THE CALIFORNIA GOLD RUSH OF 1849

DURING the course of some recent studies in the early history of printing in California, I encountered a piece of evidence regarding typographical labor organization dating back almost to the beginning of newspaper publishing in San Francisco, and throwing light on what was undoubtedly the first typographical union on the Pacific Coast. Unfortunately, we have a record of the employer's side of the question only, but we can read between the lines and glean from it much information regarding the labor situation in California at the time of the great gold rush of '49 and during a few succeeding years.

At one time, the rush of men to the mines was so frantic that there was not a newspaper being printed in California, for the simple reason that no labor was obtainable, every printer—as well as almost every other able-bodied man in the state—having gone off in search of gold. In a circular issued by the 'Californian' on May 29, 1848—it could not be called an issue—we find this amusing but significant notice, in which the publisher takes leave of his readers:

"The majority of our subscribers and many of our advertising patrons have closed their doors and places of business, and left town, and we have received one order after another conveying the 'pleasant' request that 'the printer will please stop my paper' or 'my advertisement, as I am about leaving for the Sacramento.' We have also received information that very many of our subscribers in various parts of the country have left their usual places of abode and gone to the gold region, showing that this fever (to which the cholera is a mere bungler in the way of depopulating towns) is not confined to San Francisco alone. We really do not believe that for the last ten days anything in the shape of a newspaper has received five minutes' attention from any one of our citizens. This, it must be allowed, is decidedly encouraging. The whole country, from San Francisco to Los Angeles, and from the sea shore to the base of the Sierra Nevadas, resounds with the sordid cry of "gold, Gold, GOLD!" while the field is left half planted, the house half built, and everything neglected but the manufacture of shovels and pickaxes, and the means of transportation to the spot where one man obtained $128 worth of the real stuff in one day's washing, and the average for all concerned is $20 per diem; for such, in fact, are the reports which have reached us, and from apparently reliable sources."

When the first wave of excitement subsided to a slight degree and it became possible to obtain some assistance in the printing offices, the rate of pay was determined by the scale of wages for working the mines, which was, of course, exceedingly high. The prevailing wage in the gold fields was $16 a day and the printers at work in San Francisco received, therefore, a like amount for an average day's work, which was evidently computed to be eight thousand ems daily at $2 per thousand ems.

When the gold rush spent itself, when fortunes had been made by a few and everything lost by a multitude of others, and when the labor competition with the mines became less acute, the California newspaper publishers sought some concessions from the schedule of rates of pay established under highly abnormal conditions.

The 'Alta California,' published at San Francisco, was at that time the leading newspaper of the state. It was born of the union of the two pioneer newspapers of California—the 'Californian' which had been established at Monterey in 1846 and later moved to San Francisco, and the 'California Star' which had begun regular publication at San Francisco early in 1847 under the auspices of Samuel Brannan, who had projected its issue before he left New York, and had brought the plant with him.

In the fall of 1850, by a concerted action of the publishers, rates of pay were reduced twenty-five per cent, that is, to $1.50 per thousand ems. This led to the organization of a society of compositors, which represents beyond doubt the birth of typographical unionism on the Pacific Coast.

The story is set forth in a long statement by the publishers of the 'Alta California' in the issue of that newspaper of October 28, 1851. I regret I am not able to state the other side of the case nor even to throw any light on the eventual outcome of the controversy. Perhaps some student of organization history can contribute some further information on this point.

All that I can say is that the 'Alta California' did not long retain its position of supremacy in the newspaper field. From a prosperous and powerful journal it changed in a couple of years to an impecunious one, through a series of difficulties of one kind or another—of which, perhaps its labor controversy may have been one. At any rate, early in 1855, this newspaper property was sold in bankruptcy.

Tracy, in his 'History of the Typographical Union' says that a typographical union existed in San Francisco in 1850, but that there is no information as to when it was founded. Here we have at least some definite data regarding the time of foundation and the circumstances attending the organization of the Pacific Typographical Society. In reading of the controversy in San Francisco, it is interesting, by way of comparison, to recall that the rate established at the time by the union in New York City was 32 cents per thousand ems.

As the article in the 'Alta California' may thus prove a document of fundamental importance in the history of typographical unionism in America, I am here reprinting it in full, for the first time since its original appearance in 1851.

THE PACIFIC TYPOGRAPHICAL SOCIETY AND THE ALTA CALIFORNIA

THE late action of the proprietors of this newspaper, in exercising the right of controlling their own business in their own way, having created some degree of interest among industrial classes, and led to considerable discussion, we shall make a succinct statement of our connection with and the conduct of the Pacific Typographical Society. Having done so, we shall leave the matter to the judgment of those who choose to consider it, and continue to prosecute and control our own business.

The proprietors of this journal gave employment to the first printers ever employed in San Francisco. The prices paid were in accordance with the rates of other labor, and arose in a corresponding ratio with everything else, under the impetus given to all industry by the discovery of gold; the printers themselves, like other mechanics, fixing the rates at which they worked.

In August, 1849, this office, paid two dollars per thousand ems to its workmen. In the month of January ensuing, the Tri-Weekly Alta California was merged into a daily paper, and a regular set of hands engaged in its office. Most of these printers have been employed by the office ever since. The pay of a printer in those times was proportionate with the high prices paid for every other species of mechanical labor — at the rate of two dollars per thousand ems; a good compositor, who could average about eight thousand, making sixteen dollars per day. This price seemed to be regulated to about the average per diem yield of the mines in the spring of 1850.

Two or three new papers had come into existence by the fall of 1850, and a lively competition sprung up between the job offices of each. Printers became plenty in the city, and it was soon ascertained that the usual resort of hard-pressed employers was had to cheapening labor and reducing the expenses of their business. There were no "standard rates" excepting such as had been established by the office of this paper; and when the office of the Pacific News began to be filled with what, in the patois of the profession, are termed rats, or those who work at a less price than the ruling rate, and when, in consequence, the prices charged for printing were reduced at that office, and the business of other proprietors made to suffer, a meeting of publishers was held to determine standard rates for advertising, and also to fix the rates of pay for those in their employ. This movement incensed the regular hands in all the offices, and a meeting was held, at which they resolved not to abate the prices of labor, and voted all printers to be rats who should work for less than they had received. By the same rule, however, which had determined their prices to be "standard rates" the new tariff arranged by the employers became the "regular price," and workmen were engaged at this. The reduction was 25 per cent.

A great deal of opposition was stirred up and the new hands alike with the employers were assailed with bitterness and insult. The old hands organized a society and adopted the old prices allowed by the employers, as the standard rates. In a few weeks after the change of men, one of the offices that had been less fortunate in obtaining printers, gave notice to the others that it had taken back its old hands with the old rates of pay now fixed by association. Upon hearing this, the publishers of this journal, although they did not recognize the right of the association to dictate terms, rather than incur the stigma of a low priced office, took back their old printers and agreed to pay what had now become "association rates." This association now took the name of the Pacific Typographical Society.

From this period, about September, 1850, to the month of July, 1852, nearly two years, the "ruling rates" of printing offices in 1849 were, together with rules of the most stringent character regulating the system of work for the several offices, and when and how its members should be paid, rigidly enforced by the Society. In vain the publishers remonstrated against the longer continuance of rates of labor known only in the most extravagant times of the country; in vain they petitioned, in vain sought the co-operation of the society in establishing rates fair alike for the employer and employed, — the society controlled the best workmen in the city, they knew their power and they were determined to use it. They had published a manual of Society rules, List of Prices, etc., increased their numbers by enlisting every newly arrived printer whom they could induce to join them, and really enjoyed the only independence and profit accruing from the profession in this city. Once the publishers of newspapers assembled in Convention to adopt a scale of advertising prices, which should be uniform, and the better to facilitate their plan, they invited the Society to unite with them, sign agreements, and thus establish a mutual protection against the evil effects of too much competition unlicensed as much of it was by the laws of trade. This offer was loftily rejected.

In the month of July, 1852, the proprietors of this journal, finding remonstrance and entreaties unavailing, determined to risk all upon a venture. In the language we employed at that time, in speaking of the Association, we had long desired to reduce our rates of advertising and job work, so that we might find, in an increased amount of work, an active and useful occupation for our large facilities for turning our work rapidly, well, and cheaply; but the Typographical Society have steadily and stubbornly refused to listen to our demands for a reduction in the price of labor. It was in vain that we demonstrated to them that such a course must infallibly overwhelm the employers, and eventually utterly destroy the trade — they were resolute and insolent.

We advertised for printers to take the place of the hands then employed. This had the effect of forcing the Society to meet and reduce their rates. Probaly our movement was unexpected and found the Society somewhat disorganized, therefore not immediately prepared to prevent our engaging men at reduced prices. To this we have attributed our success in the venture. We accepted the new tariff, which was the same for which we had asked two years before, and immediately, being now enabled to do so, reduced our rates of advertising, the Association hands continuing in the office.

But though the Society had reduced the prices of "plain composition" 25 per cent, they took care to provide a new source of profit in their situations. It is the custom of some morning paper offices in the Atlantic cities to pay their hands for standing idle— that is, for any considerable time which they may be "standing" after the time at which they commence composition, a charge per hour to be allowed. This rule was not among the "rules and regulations" of our most perfect Pacific Typographical Society prior to July, 1852. It then was adopted, and employers were called upon to pay the hands $1.25 for every hour which they stood idle when engaged on piece-work. Thus, while they reduced the rates of type setting 25 per cent, they insisted upon being paid for standing. A miserable scrawl, informally handed into our office, announced this decree of the Society, together with the reduction from $2 per thousand ems, or 16 dollars per day, to $1.50 per thousand, and as much pay for time unemployed as the bills, at the charge of $1.25 per hour, would call for at the end of the week.

It was the practice of the printers in this office to commence composition on the morning paper, at 7 o'clock on the night previous. The time required to set up the paper was usually about eight hours, and the composition was divided among nine men. It is frequently the case — most frequently in this city — that advertisements and the most important matter for the next day, do not come in until near midnight. But there could be no waiting, when we adjudged that space would be required, and therefore held back "copy,"—the hands must be employed or their time in which they stood paid roundly for. Such was the condition of our office at that period, regarding its supplies of type, that matter for subsequent use could not be set up without a risk of running short of letter, we were therefore compelled to pay time charges, though we sought and suggested to our printers various expedients to avoid standing,—and accepted and agreed to propositions from their foreman, which would, he promised, do away with delay. At length, after various unsuccessful endeavors to get over the difficulty, conforming to every suggestion of the printers, even to our detriment and disadvantage, we protested against the principle of time charging, situated as our office was, though we recognized it as a rule of the Society, but having made every concession, and finding it oppressive and unfair, we remonstrated against the exaction so strenuously insisted upon by some of the men, and finally referred back a bill for time, to one of the printers, declining to allow it at the time of its presentment. This was Saturday night.

On the succeeding Monday or Tuesday every man in the office resigned his situation without other explanation than that they must abide by the rules of the Association. It was about 12 o'clock in the day when they left. We advertised that afternoon for compositors, but precautions had been taken by the old hands against the filling of their situations by others —insidious stories had been circulated, and the potent cry of rat raised. No printers could be had in the city. Night came, and we were compelled to re-engage our old hands, who remained in the office under Association rules until they were dismissed last week and the present printers installed, who do not belong to the Association. Here now is the whole history of our connection with the Typographical Society of San Francisco. We have chosen to separate ourselves from such a society, and employ whom we choose to fill our office. We engaged our printers abroad because the Society had ruled the profession in this city with an iron rod. Situations were only accessible to the favored few. One set of men had filled the several offices of the city, with scarcely any variation, ever since they were established. It was impossible for a poor printer to obtain a situation except through these lucky fellows, who held their places by a sort of proprietorship. Publishers are not permitted to hire and discharge their printers, "by the rules of the Society."

These fellows would sometimes talk of "protection" — "protection to employers and the trade." Their theory was, that high prices would prevent competition, and preserve the open field to present publishers. How admirable was their "protection" we have seen in the growth of job offices in our city, in some of which, the work has been done by the proprietors, members of the profession, and who could afford to execute work at fifty per cent less than we who hired at the association rates. This is truly "the protection that vultures give to lambs."

But the half is not told. The half of arrogance, impudence and tyrannous exercise of Society rights, they have been the lords of the printing offices, dictating their own terms, and regulating their own work. We could only approach them, (and very unsuccessfully, as it is shown,) by respectful suggestions. We bore their tyranny as long as it could be borne, and until we could free ourselves from it. Their own conduct forced us to discharge them and employ others who, while receiving the same compensation as their predecessors received, are willing that we shall have some voice in the management of our own business, and who are disposed to be governed by the rules of justice and a firm regard for the rights of others. In making this change we conceive that we have exercised a right inherent in every man to employ whom he chooses in the prosecution of his business. The men whom we have dismissed from their places, have made a strenuous effort to prejudice this paper in the estimation of the craft and of the public, by misrepresentation and abuse. Having paid them for their services at the rates and under regulations fixed by themselves, we can afford to let them take their own course. We are at last independent of them and shall endeavor to remain so.

www.ingramcontent.com/pod-product-compliance
Lightning Source LLC
Chambersburg PA
CBHW061349040426
42444CB00011B/3164